BROAD MEADOW BIRD

15 Years of Poetry

Brad Vogel

First Edition, First Printing, 2015
ISBN-10: 0692441085
ISBN-13: 978-0692441084

Euphrosine Publishing
B. Vogel
220 E 29th Street
Apt. 6C
New York, NY 10016

Cover design: Suresh Seneviratne and Brad Vogel (Photo of dove and the stupa Ruwanwelisaya at Anuradhapura, Sri Lanka, B. Vogel)

Interior Artwork:
Specter (Love Songs from the Closet) – Logan De La Cruz
Water Lily (Zen) – Tracy Schwartz
Pronghorn (Surviving the Salt Mines) – Tracy Schwartz
Shell Art (Feathers) – Brad Vogel, drawings on ostrich, emu and rhea eggshells
Broad Meadow Bird (Crazy Talk) – Adelma Rasch, "End of the Corridor", B. Vogel collection
Skull (Clues) – Logan De La Cruz
Poet Photo – Suresh Seneviratne

Back cover: Suresh Seneviratne and Brad Vogel (Photo of pigeon at Hells Gate, East River, Manhattan during Rimwalk 2015, B. Vogel)

Printed in the United States of America

For M & G, who saved my life

With special thanks to Mom, Mrs. Pat Scholz, Karl Elder, my Suresh, Ms. Basting, Phil Edwards, Yousuf Siddiqui, Nate Jones, R. Booth Fowler, Melissa Nilles, the Menagerie crew, Joan Koebel, my grandparents, Matt Cline, Mike Mathes, Stacey Jeanty, D, my siblings, Kelly Jelinek, Logan De La Cruz, Jake J, the Man in the Hat, Ms. Schlemmer, Tracy Schwartz, Benedict Campbell, Paul Lozito, Serena Kuo, Fritz Koeppen, Adinah's Farm on Avenue C, the Sheboygan County Writer's Club, the Kiel Public Library, a coffeeshop in Austin, Texas, the Lester Public Library, the Terrace, the ghosts of Robinson Jeffers, Ellen Kort and Lorine Niedecker and all my muses.

Thanks, too, to the support of 78 Kickstarter backers who helped make this book a reality.

"it was safer not to go off before I'd fulfilled a sacred duty,

by making verses and thus obeying the dream"

CONTENTS

I.

Love Songs From the Closet

White Hot

Stage Fright

H_2O

Fell as a Bullet

St. Charles Line

Industrial Strength

"Sing Then the Core"

Sumac Sutra

Overgrown

Kingfisher

Z Train

Ouzel

"Opium Den"

Mad Props to a Visiting Rousseau Scholar

Inside Two Weeks

II.

Zen

Blue Jay

July

Chief

Fire Wheels Whir

Living

Encapsulating Time

Goblin Valley

Bell Captain's Stand

44th, Vanderbilt, and Madison

Spring

The Bittersweet Mysteries

Something Borrowed

Fire Danger High

Blackout Clash

Hall of Remembrances

From a Tower in Hong Kong

Picking Stones

Mocha Velvet Bottlebrush

Written in the Dark

Manitowoc

Iris

Alpha-Omega

Nachtmusik

Late

Mellification

III.

Feathers

Cry of the Indigo Bunting

Montgolfier

Diamonds

Having Met Life

Indelible Tea (In the Pines)

Strangled

By Water

Marsh

Neutral Ground Runners

Carefully Scruffy

Smoke

Tamarack

Eine Cline

Red Ostrich Feathers in the Living Room

Quake Before the Lord

IV.

Surviving the Salt Mines

Where There is Smoke

Terminal City

42nd Floor

Never Touch the Stuff

Too Many Irons Smother A Fire

FOB, Fear of Breaking

March at the Firm

Prayer to My Patron

Charon's Yellow Skiff

November

Progress

Succession

Inner Plateau

Kilimanjaro

Tunnel's End

V.

Crazy Talk

Orange

The Health Benefits of Temporary Insanity

A Defense of Love

Semi-Abstract Angry Musings

Speed

Cedar Waxwing

Egg Nog

Hound Dog Tayloring Along

Bird 1506

POSH

Big Golden

Dog Days

Swig

Cheating Death

Be Not Afraid

What General Jackson Saw

Red Shift

Isle Hustle

Room, The Slanty Shanty

Curtains

~ CLUES ~

About the Poet

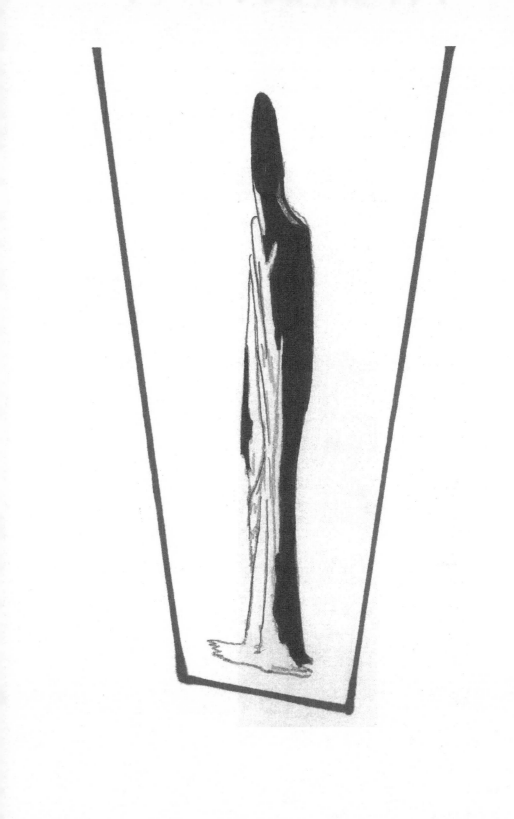

LOVE SONGS FROM THE CLOSET

White Hot

The lines under my eyes
Are the queues to see you,
My crowsfeet the tracks
Of a bird who wants to fly

I woke up for you this morning,
The sky finally blue
And nothing more

Perhaps it was the day I noticed
My jeans hanging loose
Or maybe the same hour my
Vision went peripheral-only

But it was there
Shortly after the love songs
Clicked, the generic pronouns
Took on a face, a smile –

It's a long way
Even as the crow flies

I hurtle back from orbit
Ablaze, wide-eyed as the shield
Burns away, disintegrates

Orange, blue
White hot

Tears vaporized
Upon re-entry

Stage Fright

Consider this my second line –
The first will not appear tonight
Thanks to lack of courage

Read it
In the knocking of my knees
The mischief lounging in my eyes

H₂0

When the final drop boils away
Basin rocks fevered with steam,
The jagged ridges uncomfortably red, stinking
Coated with carapace,
Sizzling tentacles, moisture
Escaping the last whale's
Blowhole sigh, requiem
For an ocean, a world

I will tear open the hatch
Roaring,
Broiling, raging forward
Down glittering avenues
Searing with each pink step
Reeking of ground chuck
I will find you yet

Seated, musing in the highest tower
Surveying a torrid ghost realm:
Barnacled spires
Marvelous halls
    -    a city unveiled at last
And I will stagger up the staircase
Fin-cut, shell-shocked

Out of the sulfurous trench

Reeling and salt-brained

Wretching, cursing

Into your arms

Atlantis

Fell as a bullet

I needed you, lines
words
Grasped desperately at dock's edge
for metaphors

So smooth, ossified
great griplessness on parade
like the cumulus piles above
   -   that were all I had
page after page
no toeholds
fingers shredded
   -   they and bleached blue
dead drumbeat too
   mute beat of my heart

I needed you, lines
to tether me
tie me to my barely-extant, tossed out luggage
throw me a semicolon at least;

Hold me
til the ferry comes

Well sometimes I go out by myself
and I look across the water
and find no consolation
in verse or sky

No lines, no lines

Some fools would eat poetry
- and I tried -
but I knew then
as one last swan coasted by
final page turned up blank as a cloud

and the ferry hove to
     -    It wasn't over
but it was over

I'll write my own lines
bound in my adventuring

I write to kill

St. Charles Line

Onyx men clip lawn
Beneath Robert E. Lee
As we circle, sweating,
Screeching into the Warehouse District
Sharp white pillar, bellowing sun

I play a streetcar role
The suit who bails at Poydras
Uptown carpetbagger
   -   Who's poorer than you
Desperately wanting to talk

But we do not talk
And a sour darkness grew
In the shade of my half-response
In light of our callousness

Wooden seats and open windows
   -   These are my hope
That I might congeal again somehow
Wrapped in humidity, pressed tight
Gasping for repairs that require being broken

Two engines out,
One aflame
Fuel tanks shot through
No wires overhead
And yet aloft
As if gravity, for a moment
Forgot

Industrial Strength

She swings her words

Like rusted pick axes

They lodge in the ribs,

Crusty rhino horns

Rooting for my heart.

"Sing Then the Core"

Death comes in little boxes
Lacquered black, cobalt blue
Unstackable, slightly rounded
Piled nevertheless

I would hide them in the attic,
Stash them in the garage,
Mound them on the kitchen table
   -   but I do not have these things

Death comes in little boxes
And keeps on coming
Smoothest sandalwood
Perfectly dovetailed

I would squeeze them in the closet
But it is already bursting

Death comes in little boxes
Delicately, silently hinged
Fitting mouse-like
In the palms of my hands

I have their jaws shut
Those little yawning maws
   -   every last goddamn one

Little boxes chew their death
Bovine, herding, heaping in the hallway
I wade through them
Toward the door

Death comes in little boxes
Like this
The one you made for me

Sumac Sutra

Staghorn burns red
Licks interstate overpasses
Stings my eyes
With the smoke
Of longing, a trust,
A life generally
Deferred
- I am driving myself
-

Hues mark the time
Muffler counts miles
That I am away
From one mind
Who has never closed the door
- I am still
-

The destination is the passenger
I see through drooping bloodshot eyes
- When I finally arrive
-

Some loves
Have compound leaves

Overgrown

Only say the word

And I shall be healed

Leaves rasp in my throat

- This thing has germinated

Grown inside

Vines unfurling in the dark warmth

Tendrils corkscrew down

The inside of capillaries

- I am overrun with foliage

Blossoms push

At the back of my lips

Kingfisher

I like your fauxhawk,
Kingfisher
Your cry, too,
I cannot ignore

Though I paddle on
Staring straight ahead
Trying not to look
At the splendid specimen
Hopscotching along
Lighting up my insides –

You leave me waiting
For the next wild willows
My canoe must pass

Z Train

A rushing

A creaking of rust-hued feathers

And there you are

A rare bird I hardly knew existed

As unlikely as a burrowing owl

Appearing out of the darkness

Approaching Bowery stop

A little tingle in the entrails

A look, a look, another look

A tentative step into ethereal talons

A wonder you are here

And so am I

A whisper-winged day

A ride to remember

Ouzel

Hide, then
With waterfall shields
Cliff ferns, a craggy gorge

Secret yourself
By glacial streams
In mountain fastness

Years pass
Time caresses boulders
Falls

But there you are
Undeniable
Stone gray

Gray as a monk
Droplets beaded
Featherwise

Gingerly stride a branch
- bold for such a thing
March into mountain flood

Eyes flashing, intent
Underwater tremolo
- you can't be unseen

My one aquatic songbird

"Opium Den"

From "Swan Song or Life Thus Far"

Bottle, boxes, pepperoni, paraphernalia
Every one disintegrated yet part of the scheme

Each moment and whatever happens thrills me with joy
I loaf and invite my soul,
I lean and loaf at my ease observing a game of Super Smash.

I, now twenty-two years old in perfect health begin,
Hoping to cease not till I can live.

I celebrate myself, and sing myself
Pulling away from shore, having
Play'd the part that still looks back on the actor or actress
The same old role, the role that is what we make it, as great
as we like
Or as small as we like, or both great and small

I am
Hidden in the tall grass,
- I love everyone more than I'm willing to admit –
The meat department
In Ginsburg's California supermarket

You have waited, you always wait
We fathom you not – we love you – there is perfection in you
also
Here inebriated under starry white lights,
Sloping wooden ceiling,
Incense drifting from a wooden Tiki man
Battered couches

O throat! O throbbing heart!
And I singing uselessly, uselessly all night
The aria sinking
The strange tears down the cheek coursing
From the memories of the bird that chanted to me

I, chanter of pains and joys

Sing on, you gray-brown bird.
Sing from the swamps, the recesses, pour your chant from the
bushes,
Ceaselessly musing, venturing, throwing, seeking the spheres
to connect them,
Till the bridge you will need be form'd,
Till the ductile anchor hold
Till the gossamer thread you fling catch somewhere

O, my soul

Mad Props to a Visiting Rousseau Scholar

Bright eggnog glasses
I sip right along
Stasis hearthside

We heart our chains
Festooning each limb
As with garland

What a pretty presentation
How appropriate
A cozy evergreen

But you crash the party
Spill hot mulled cider
Don't give a damn

I blush, aunts faint
You cast them off, grinning
Tickled by needles

Standing bare daring
Steel link piles wreath your feet
Eyes flipping the bird

They stare, full bound
Hint of a smile
I look down, pick at red giftwrap

Corner of my eyes
    -    no one else notices –
You're under the mistletoe
One defiant jaybird

Looking
@#!%& sexually attractive
    -    Now THIS is a citizen!

Inside Two Weeks

Down, under 4,000 feet of rock
My legs are failing me

Someone has left a plasma torch
Sparking white at the end of the tunnel

And it is you
And I do not know if I will make it

Five months have I run
In frozen stone

Toward fixed microscopic subterranean star
The speck of light hitting your pupil

I am driven on, entering
Mile 26 – the darkness hides the bleeding

And yet you blaze
And I sprint to immolation

Burn these cords that bind me
O heat, O light

ZEN

Blue Jay

I barely glimpsed

A bursting blue blur

Indigo ICBM

Sodalite rocket

Whizzing, whirring, flying;

- Faster than Owen Hart -

Spanning the "thread of life"

(Crusher of life)

A winged sky shard

Alighting on vibrant sumac

Escaping the hurtling

Blue Bird I sit in

Seeing what no one else saw:

Vivid autumn fresco

Intricate to the point of simplicity

In the dusky sunlight –

I was conscious

For a moment.

July

searing black bulge of inflatable Shamu

pressing up against your tummy by the grill

under leafy lakeside veranda

    -    the mind is a swallowtail;

the fate of the world

hangs in the balance of a volleyball game

Chief

I, here in the belly of a cloud

Am envious of your jealousy.

I wish I could wish that I were here,

For I sit as a brick frosted over,

I, here in the empty moonlight.

Give me a crown of moonbeams,

For I am lord of all

That is naught.

Let it scintillate here in cold, stark guts.

I, here in the elliptical ranch of supremacy,

Shake hands and force a grin

With shrieking gray-eyed

Souls

As they check out

Again and again and again.

Fire Wheels Whir

Kerosene bright
White night elephants
Silver jasmine
Flames

Whip crack drum slap pipe drone chimes
Tears

Tuskers dance
Sway in smoke
Blaze

Time quavers
Ripples away
Radiant

Kandyian night
Alight

Living

April had just left

Whitewashing bank stones

With a Palladian rigor

As the last carp harem

Heaved itself into the pools

Under foamy, mint-hued willow buds

That swayed

 In waltzing, sun-sugared scent

Which air-fresheners too often imitate

In vain,

While I hooked the nightcrawler

Three times

- And re-signed the contract

With the light of my eyes

Encapsulating Time

    Hand me the butterfly net
That I might capture this day
As it flits and darts
In thick, baking rays of sun,
Rays that bleach fly-clad sheephead
Half-wrapped in smothering wet sand,
Glinting in the torrid afternoon.

Pass me the stringer
That I might get this moment through the gills
With its swing dancing swallows,
Carefree as laughter from the cottage deck,
Swooping, radiant,
Weaving over bright, oscillating wave tips,
Forked tails plugged into the outlet of day.

Lend me a camera
That I might preserve this instant,
Its billion zebra mussel tea set;
Sharp porcelain piles in biting hot surf,
Feet keeping negatives for development,
Shots of caressing breezes, warm algal waves,
And tickly grass in hammock shadows.
Mostly, though, faces unhitching wagons.

Give me a pen

That I might live this once again

Years from now, yellowed

- I will recall this swarm of 61,701 gnats about me –

No oriole, Halloween harbinger, will slip unnoticed

Amongst waxy leaves of the oak grove,

Trunks columnar as saurian femurs,

Solid as the sticky-shirted clan

That lounges sunblasted at their bases.

That I might cram it full

With bottle rocket remnants,

Secondhand small-horse outboards,

Oblong black pebbles,

Freshly-mown grass, sun tan lotion,

And snapshots of seconds

Ensconced in polish glass

With all quarks on "charm".

Clustered bubbles roll happily, fleetingly now, as foam on the
bay.

Bring me iridescent solution, friend,

That I might tease forth these glistening spheres

To encapsulate time.

Goblin Valley

Who do I long for -
You, blue fade Utah
Silent sunscarp stone trees

Weird corridor strolls
Mind goes moonboot bouncing
Socks in sandals, siblings half-seen

   -    vacuum, stifled scream
blasting by the exit
90 miles per hour

For one small step...!

Landerless leaden stomach stare
Orbit childhood, never touch down
Decades of mumbo jumbo will hoodoo you

Rock flags planted still
Footprints in powder, no wind
Million miles away

Bell Captain's Stand

Patience in green scales the gables

Wrapping gingerly about a ledge now

Each move deliberate, premeditated

Up turret heights it climbs

And I am dawn in –

Twining, growing, contemplating

Blanketing the rigid hulk

Ethereally in a soft glow

Up and up I follow from the trellis

My sight engrossed

I weave in with eager tendrils

Into leafy recesses high above

I try to step away

I thrash now like a fly in a web

Unable to see

Myself

Now trapped......

The siding sizzles today

Like molten marble

Vines can be heard growing

In a small crsh-wieck, crsh-wieck........

44th, Vanderbilt, and Madison

Yale Club......Yale Club.....
Roosevelt Hotel......

Flurries scale brick and glass gulches
Whirling up
Snowing from sidewalk to sky

I find it strangely comforting
That they, too
Get tossed about
Pulled in zany trajectories
By Midtown midday mayhem

We snowglobe brothers
Frantically going
Yet oddly calm

Suckers for a wild ride

Spring

Sparrows shot furiously

Out of the shrubbery

Like rounds from a Tommy gun,

Godmother Nature's shock weapon

Wreaking vengeance on the neighborhood

For the murder

Of her cold-hearted nephew,

Jackie Frost

The Bittersweet Mysteries

Church committees will be the death of me,
what with their veneer of opening
prayer and all,
the soundless maneuvering
like crocs navigating mangrove roots
(for an increase in the virtue of patience)
- St. Isidore was lucky
enough to have an angel grip
oaken plow handles,
splinters driving home,
while we are stuck
with these labors
dealing in leaky air conditioners and
women chaplains
or the lack thereof;
crucifix,
stapler,
monstrance,
Xerox:
A harsh light whips
back and forth
and I am knocked from my horse
on the road to the capitol...
for the parish is
(mantra, mantra)
more than a building,
but buttresses
on occasion
butt in,
incensing
the congregation,
the committee,
the confirmandees
of a faith in spreadsheets
- our life, our sweetness, and our hope -
even now as

my fingers hum
along the beads
dripping down my forehead
plooching into the baptismal font
with a roar
that warrants a secretarial note
in the minutes
she takes them longhand,
sucking pink gummi savers – our
daily bread –
from her ring finger
like an anteater after ants
offhandedly
silhouetted in stained glass
shadows thrown by the tabernacle light
that tells me he is still here
though dim
and maybe
every candle needs its wax
and that is why I am here
doing my Job
broiling, uncomfortable
crowding the wick
being consumed by
the fifth and final Bittersweet Mystery, The Realization
is not man's life on earth
a drudgery
when drippings pile the
sconce
slippery, spent
me
      -     lead me not into temptation
but deliver me from evil
save us from the fires of Hell
and lead all souls to Heaven
pillar of ivory
may perpetual light shine upon you
(move to adjourn)

St. Sebastian sits in his cheap chair
as the final arrow hits home and,
gasping
he seconds

In nomine Patris et Filii et Spiritus Sancti
Amen

Something Borrowed

Palms, hammocks and aloe light

Harsh dry be-speckled mountains

Oranges roll under lush hedges

White chairs for the wedding

The chortle of a fountain

A little girl's laugh

So far away

Barely a breeze

Fire Danger High

Who knew water could be so dry:
There are days when packed air
Condensates into sparrows
Dust droplets flicking in the sun
A shrill cheep-wit crackling out

There are times when blasted junipers
Undulate, rasping with green scales
Breaking on caked, drab hillsides
An Oread

There are moments when an hourglass
Releases its flow over the brink
Sending a torrent with a silent roar
Into the next cloud

It falls again
Into my waiting mouth

Blackout Clash

That night, the wayward Fate
Would wear black
    Black as the interior of bones.
She slammed a might monkey wrench
In the flywheel of humanity
    "Fireflies will do tonight,"
I heard whispered amidst approaching thunderclaps.
I grinned, tasting drowned worms,
As she donned her gown.

Down the way, flickers sprouted in
Oily windows – not mine.

    Solid as granite, I sat unseen
Humid in a rocker.
Go on and be flustered, go on, foolish colts.
I sat jubilant, victorious, counting
Pregnant blackberries
Through the porch rail with my
Toes.

Hall of Remembrances

D.C. 2001

The burning bush – I saw it –
About 100 yards up the sidewalk
From the Bureau of Engraving and Printing.

There it was, burning but not consuming.

If God spoke, it was too hard to hear
With the cement trucks careening
Down the wide avenue,
Trumpeting air brakes like
Pachyderm Philistines

We were leaves on the burning bush
  -   I saw it –

Surrounded by the spirit,
But yet untouched.

From a Tower in Hong Kong

"nuclear radiation or acts of God"

what is the difference
I asked myself
As hawks rolled past
Neighboring skyscrapers

And I looked down on the Harbor
    -    At everything –
With over-wide, circular
Jardine eyes

"Thank you, mate."

And I was back to the Macanese matter
Wondering if I should call Chlorophyll Yip
Just for the fun of it

Picking Stones

Some tasks remain human;
In the end
Bits don't budge boulders

So a small drab band hunts and pecks
Hoisting granite and limestone
Annually worn by
And proud of their accomplishments
Annually returning to their rocks,
To their futile labor

The farmer
A Sisyphus
Harvesting his endless bumper crop
Of sprouting bedrock

Muddy jeans shuffle down furrows
As the wagon jolts on with its burden
Creaking ever forward

mocha velvet bottlebrush

Mullein leaves serve up their Swarovski buffet
four does, bound tightly, bound by
making small sounds
tickling leaves

What is wind and what is river?
the hush so calm and stilled the band can barely play
every slow motion ripple
a premonition billowing out

Great arcing necklaces undone
heaving chests
the chains liquefy
gem convoys laze downstream

Sumac clouds and swallows
dawn comets
unadorned

Too fleeting, too brief
like my standing here now
steroids waning already
we will soon be back in the city

But I saw four deer
from a strange unseen angle
wondered as their hips worked
if they're more mocha velvet bottlebrush
or exactly the hue
of all these boulders
gracefully migrating
waltzing
downstream

Written in the Dark

Lunch in the garden
Tinged with Camelot
Light through trees
Casual conversation
Ivy and wrought iron
Woodsmoke

We all danced on the heads of pins

He says he never has known music
But the hymns he whistles on occasion
I can tell –
He is good

Manitowoc

Seagulls floating over the factory

Whistling a Cake song

Aviators on

-    it told of an ancient radiation

Whipping lit at doors

Like throwing stars

Unfolding blue white red

Spread eagle on the welcome mat

Sun, yellow shirt

Sidewalk

Blue sky

Hot water heater

On the curb

I yearn for

Frappuccino

Iris

Stately ornate masterpiece
Sunshine-throated vase
Twilight-colored canopies
Draping golden lace

Slender silver-greenish stem
Leaves that dance in dew
Hidden in a marshy cove
Perfect violet view

Living ruffled amethyst
Fit for a bouquet
Stooped, then stopped above the bloom –
I'd pick some other day.

Alpha – Omega

So this is what it's like:
This comfortingly calm assuredness
The unexpected warmth
Vision suddenly clarifying
Our pain my pain
Into a ball of soft white light
Everything's in its right place;
I am walking through waving grain
The field laps the feet of
Family I haven't seen so long
Time reiterates itself in subtle ways
The clock face in Library Mall winks
The curtains are flung open
Dust flies, joy streams in
She shifts from leg to leg
Across the hall
Simple pleasures consuming
The gray matter once
Devoted all too much to breathing
So comforting this leaf loam
The air glows an autumnal orange-brown
Rich, full, content
Acorns stashed safely

Nachtmusik

1:01

1:02

Moonlight Sonata descending

Haunting

Nail clipper unused

Printer humming

Rocking out pages

Ivy un-watered in shadow

Blurry with contacts out

Paper stacks

Blinds closed

Clothes piled

Underwear

Back bent

Ludwig here at the desk

Scratching on Poli Sci letterhead

Bulbs become wicks

Candles in the room

Notes fade

Blown out

1:08

Late

Three clocks
Jostle for my attention
Where I sit

Each a distant galaxy
Ticking or glowing
Just for me

Yet sound waves and photons
Take time – too long
For time

Info as worthless to me
As light
From the Horsehead Nebula

Dead on arrival
Celestial scrapbook
Phantom time

Mellification

One day, they got sweet
Gave up everything, went all in
Ingesting the honey of old poems

Became rock candy men
The sting came out
Stanza by viscous stanza

Their bones were simply covered
In flower pollen
And in bees' broken toes

FEATHERS

Cry of the Indigo Bunting

Dawn opens faint blue

Tremendous chicory bloom

Quick – the petals close

Montgolfier

When you feel no wind

Look down – you're with it – buck's breath

Plows iced oats, greets dawn

Diamonds

How to cut the gem
Whittle diamond with diamond
My eyes await you

Park bench at sunrise
Irises alight at last
Carve, bright shavings fly

Having Met Life

Morning march up Park
Chrysler's spire shadow retreats -
Yes, sundial, I'm late

Indelible Tea (In the Pines)

Two chameleons

Danced closer amidst shady pines

-    touched, disappeared

Strangled

Catsclaw climbs me

Yellow blooms choke sagging porches

-    Someone lives here

Propped up by scaffolding that

Grasps - tries to take me down

By water

Triptych under trees

Lorine's deck – she streams by

Horn-rims

Curls

blue

Marsh

Iced Alladin's lamp
For my skis to rub upon -
Genies in the reeds

Neutral Ground Runners

Orangutan arms

Reach out green to embrace us

- see Xs, hope Os

Carefully scruffy
Loving all provocation

Smoke

Writhe ghost dragon chain

Dissipate at conception

Breathe fire on winter

Tamarack

Tower of barbed-wire

Barren brown nervous system

Sensing frosted air

Eine Cline

Why not roll with this

February concision

Bare branches few words

Red Ostrich Feathers in the Living Room

For Janet

Ms. Ella is gone now

Gone to Cambronne

Ms. Ella who lived in the golden shotgun

Quake Before the Lord

Woodsmoke for incense

Silence

The crackle of the stove

A voice

Oak leaves flickering in wavy glass

SURVIVING THE SALT MINES

Where There is Smoke
For Karl Elder

Dark pipe-fueling silhouette
A great-horned owl
He fills this spine-lined nest

Looming in the window branches
Clinging somehow to naked trees
Piercing submarine November blue

    -   I have never met this man
And he will not turn on the light
So I stay in my coat and we go on by embers

Talking of the tripe, but also
My Thanatopsis, a perfect zen poem
And whether sodalite is too esoteric

I am Nineteenth Century he says
I am 100 years behind
Surely, I must have read Walcott?

For I used only redtail
And the final line is appropriately ambiguous
(Which I hadn't even known)

This little country college
Has a man who spouts Pound
Makes milk truck bazookas

The professor sees I can make it new
The rusticated cocoa and mahogany voice
Tells me the poet sees the spark, there's fire

    -   And I made a choice there, unnerved in the dark
Leaving me here as he climbs God and Louis

Like Lilliputian stepladders

Leaving me to invoke in vain
St. Stevens and the emperor he conjured
That I, too, might escape my coming perch
High in some van der Roh cage.

Terminal City

She spews bitches
And assholes
From jackhammer's irate tip
Pit stains spiraling

Unclear whether the sun's out or not
Push
Shove
NYC

The anti-love

42nd Floor

2.

My heart barrels
Across cream-colored bricks
And worn plaza mortar,
A stampede of Appaloosas,
Anxiety out of control
Swallowtails flapping
In stomach enzymes.
- Nervous

11.

Though my easy grin
Lounges about,
Placid mountain tarn
  Sky-blue, at peace...

14.

Higher upslope, tension builds, though
In the silence.
The avalanche grins madly,
  Waiting to be conceived.

18.

Still, like this steely door before me
  It will open.

20.

It will roar as the hinges crack
Like shots ringing out
Thrashing the pristine tarn.
It will gallop downhill

With wild Sioux ails.
It will surge with cold venom
  As the icy vacuum belches.

25.

The inquiry perches close now
Six-legged
Antennae pulsing,
  Hungry.
    I rise.

28.

As my temperature
Radiates to melt Greenland,
  Climbs upslope
With lasso in hand.
Whirling and whipping
  Halting the herd

32.

I think of speaking to my inquisitor
  At the threshold.
And bright-winged confetti
Erupts unseen from my mouth
Having navigated esophagus,
Escaping captivity

38.

  As the steely capsule slows.
Freezing the tarn in serenity.

40.

I will gaze at its frozen reflections

Across the desk.

41.

And sense a trotting echo
Across brick-clad plaza,
  My heart in the saddle at last.

42.

"Good morning, right this way…"

Never Touch the Stuff
On arriving home from a 15-hour day at the office

Down two tabs of Niedecker
Catapulted into cattails
Riotous green
Wake at impact
4 in the morning

Night birds flock
To your splash
    -   the broken stems
Nose stings
Lines of
Methane bubbles
A wavy mirror in moonlight
The things we need.

What's it to you?
You snort petrels
Algae, reeds – I'm onto you
One of those tamarack freaks
Bags of night heron
Line your wet halls

- and mine.

Too Many Irons Smother A Fire

Pardon me while I die here for a moment
   -   It will only be a short rest

Here amidst the lily pads and methane rainbows
The cattails and disheveled duck blinds
This overripe greenness buzzing in
My now wet ears and tingling
Algae-filled nostrils – I smile weakly
Somewhere between exhaustion and relief
Descending from my cloud, its
Silver lining unraveling rapidly, unable to
Keep me from sinking into a taste of
Snapping turtle and muskrat – the harsh
Powder blue sky dangles its sun overhead
Like a nightlight for my slumber.

Now I lay me down to sleep…
On a pillow with scales, not feathers

I sigh at the spears, innumerable as reeds,
Stuck about my person –
From whom I wonder?
From me?

My life flashes, projected on a snow white
Lily bloom, its delicate petticoats barely above water

A gnat lands on the blossom now
And it is plunged beneath the surface
   -   It will only be a short rest

FOB, Fear of Breaking
§ 2–319

→ How did I end up here?
Lymph nodes flared,
Outlines and tabs and casebooks awash
1,000 miles from home
In an over-cold carrel
A great black pelican, death pelican
Glowering above?

It's funny what wells up
Amidst the fever and night sweats
And conflicting caselaw,
The undergrad girls out back
Under the gypsy-ravaged branches
At 4 am, their animal noises
Jarring me from a warranty for a particular purpose

But it's the farm
  Grandpa Isaac at age 106
  A classmate in a tawdry 1980s bathroom
  Half my butt fitting in some sort of
    Slide chute in blue tile down a hillside
  A non-existent bug that wakes me 1 minute
    Before the alarm

To the next shortness of breath
To Imperfect Acceptance
Of the place of destination

March at the Firm

A harried mind
Back-up generators for days

Teaspoons of neutron star
Teaspoon after teaspoon
Deal after deal
Getting that post-death feeling
Jello legs
Paper mountain ranges grow
Mutiny talk
In every unslept cabin

Breadfruits overboard
Jerry cans out
Sigh

Deep in the whale
I said would not swallow me

Stomach cavern dark
Doggy paddling - flail splashing
Back toward the rope

Hold on

Prayer to my Patron

O, St. Wallace
I pray that you might intercede
On this hunched back
Flourescent-lighted
Windowless one's behalf
Teeth gnashing chalky intercreditors

Swimming upstream
Black caustic inbox waters
Desperate strokes
Back to my rope
Ending here in whale gut
- The way out nearly lost

The good ones are gone
Never risked going this deep
In the belly
Where digestion creeps in

Send me ice cream, Emperor
Keep it coming, make it ridiculous
Til this skyscraper bloats at the seams
Erupts in pink granite sherds
Midtown corporate
Smithereens

Charon's Yellow Skiff

Patience and Fortitude

And scaffolding groves

Tanks and prams and

Homeless bundles; men in suits

Hubcap

Zeppelin dock

Big old iron

Pen scratches

But is not there

No sidewalk

No skyscrape here

Trundling along, poled

Apart

Dark waters home

Last lights whirl

All in a time near death

November

The part of the show when

Unseen stagehands turn on the fans

To create a hovering dry ice mist.

When the backdrop lowers

Showing dismal gray oak skeletons

And iron skies.

It's the scene where lovers'

Yearnings come to naught,

While each stares blankly down

At the dying leaves and frosted grass.

A slow, mournful requiem

Grudgingly wailed by the

String and backed with

Ghastly bass patterns

As the audience digs

Further into its seats,

Hunkering down uneasily

For the final act.

Progress

Proud cluster of silos

Rises empty over

The city's vinyl-sided arm

Obese pigeons whir out

To birdfeeders as numerous

As the bright stalks of corn, the beech trees

That once thrived

Here

Here is the cement and shingle sea

Drowning the homestead

Which has stood so long

Its fieldstone charred

By the Peshtigo fire

Here

Where black and white Holstein ghosts

Swish their tails

Against the swing sets

Succession

I

Summer's final notes
Sound like mellow pears
Thudding off scale
Into grass clef

II

The last clinging walnut
Drops as a carved iron nugget
Pounding frost-flecked mud
Of bitter November night

III

Long let me serenade
The uncertain bough
Hoarding sap and ripeness
That in descending at last
I might shade out
This falling snag I hang upon

Inner Plateau

Shock is a pronghorn

Loping tautly across

Arid neurons,

My sagebrush-speckled mind

Scrambling now

Up jagged scree fields

Climbing closer

I attempt to pick it off

But my scope is no match

And it advances through ricochets

Sweat beads appear

As I sit tensely

On this lonesome mesa

Deep in my thoughts

The antelope

Powers

Up

Its bony black knives

Carrying the news

Kilimanjaro

Hyena's outside the tent now
Cackling away, the bastard
Cackling away in the dark
I, too, see vignettes flash by
The sweet debris disinterred
Sprawled out on the snow
Or what remains, anyway
Sickly blue scraps suckling in vain
Only a barren crag
To support his mesh tent
Wracked with frigid dread
In the shadow of the wreckage
Giddy lunatic snickering
Warping, swelling, heightening
Fuselage, stone, weak moon
Paralysis in its approach

But a purple-blue hand
Thrusts out violently
And grips the pen,
Teeth grit vice-like

-    It is time to sculpt the headstones
That they might live

Tunnel's End

For Brian

My dress shoes are packed
My dress shoes and my shirt and tie
They will be needed
I am told
The funeral could be Saturday

A black ride home
Through cold drumlin fields

But she is still there
Still here on the couch
Her deathbed

When I arrive
They are amazed that she speaks;
Your hands are so cold, she says

I apologize
I do not want to be
The coming of death
To a woman too young

I have prayed for you, I say
I have thought about you a lot
But she is still again
Quiet, staring, wasting away
Inexplicably alive

What to say
How to console
A family ground down
Over two years
Resigned

I step out
Arms outstretched
Walking the tightrope

It is precarious here between
Living on,
Being smothered

Shadows hug the high walls
Always at night these things

These things so cold
That light itself
Freezes
Seems to sink from view

CRAZY TALK

Orange

Unrhymably violent

Exotic, stalking Bengal

Worn prolific in November

Like a blazing Tide

    Plucked juicily from its spokes,

Lush fragrance

From the magma sphere

    Tinting morning with warning,

Marmalade spread on dawn

Like innumerable cooked crawdads

Clinging to Zion's cliffs

    Inconsistent, unapologetic

- A Denver fan eating cheddar

On the brash roof

Of the Church at Auvers

    But citric frontiers have closed

Wild hawkweeds no longer roam,

Domesticated and ever-blaring

Road cones

The Health Benefits of Temporary Insanity

Zing!

- Kung-fu – Hiy-Yaah!

Like a crazed lobster, I'm told

I frantically whip a dull

White hunk of plastic to life,

Cracking and lashing out,

Dancing nimbly in dim light of

The Arcade.

I am Zorro and Jackie Chan

I move like The Matrix

Thrust!

Parry!

It sings, whizzing, a hot potato

Done in chartreuse plastic,

Hovering between the hyper-extended

Arms of two violently happy

Wearers of smiles and sweat.

Intensity hums audibly.

I am one with the puck…

  Back, forth

  Back, forth

I ricochet hard

From cruel sides

Where am I headed?

I am but a rocketing pawn

Tossed between two minds,

Two ivory crescents.

Faster I fly

And still more rapidly –

KLA-CHING.

A Defense of Love

1. Brilliant blue gets this rather unsavory connotation when your hair is ablaze.

2. No, I really have painstakingly whipped out the kung-fu on each rose petal and addressed every last ravenous thorn with Janet Reno's long lost high-power rifle.

3. It's Reno Time here on the dark side of the moon in a cozy back table at our Texan neighbor's seedy café. Elton John pompously butchers Johnny Cash's deathbed remake of Nine Inch Nails. Nowhere else could one so avidly ponder the plural of moose. Six cranes on the skyline – how romantic. You must've called ahead, how sweet.

4. Every time a bell rings, a corpse unthaws in the morgue. Mistletoe noose over yonder?

5. What has thou done, O duchess of angioplasty? Thy kingdom swells, a zeppelin lumbers aorta-ward. Thine own valentine falls from the sky into mouths of yearning giant Asian carp[1]. They are me and I am glad; love shall findeth a way.

6. David Koresh tiptoes through the twinkling tulips, trailing wiltedness.

---

[1] They've almost breached the gap! The horde surges against yon electric wall that braces the fair Illinois Shipping Canal. Ten Ton Tilly shall not abjure the joy of Midwestern fisherman, whipping and cavorting and thrashing so, so help me.

7. For you, too, is from the Branch Davidian Ark[2].

Indeed you are the sight of the spark and the death of the dank; you are the raven on a lark in the dank little spark; you want to disembark on the peak with the fruit (or the beak) of the raven on a lark:

8. She's the man from the Yucatan, 1971 Chevrolet chariot of flames rocketing through the Everglades, alligators flying off the hood into the mangroves like legos flung with festive abandon. You bust a gut as she blows a gasket, the odometer cartwheeling heatedly through the butt-rusted gizzard. Federal agents unleash the arsenal of democracy. I am more convinced of your commitment than ever.

9. For I have raised my Zippo to your fiber optic scalp crop and you have convinced me of meese that roam dreamily somewhere in Saskatchewan. I assume all remaining lamentations emanate from the inner chamber of your new gall bladder. Wring it dry and clutch your glasses as you burst forth again through the wall.

10. Salman Rushdie reincarnated in my Hagen Daas again! However, by the way your pinkie introduces itself to my thumb, I sense you care little, or want to be done.

11. Respect my authoritay, Janet, my beautiful blazing kingfisher o' love.

12. We Ain't Comin' Out!

---

[2] Thus, the cults shall file aboard two by two, performing elaborate rites and rituals. An experienced Chinese government official is retained to ensure adequate space for all.

Semi-Abstract Angry Musings

Fling thought like Key Lime Pie yogurt
Out of a bushel basket
From the cornice of a five story store.
Ride the wind, amoebic cowboy
Who was born in an udder
On Bill Taft's south lawn Pauline
   -   Did he or she get stuck in the tub?
And it freezes, a sea-green nebula,
Like snot in the Yukon
On this first Thursday in November,
The month of cold eyes,
Grim skies and Key Lime Pies...
     Wafting on muscle-bound breezes

Birthed by bunker buster bombs
Looking to keep the Blackhawks up
In their vigil over the Hindu Kush
Where a tiny village in the dust
Harbors a commando
     Curtis Brooks with beard
A bullet in the Taliban headgear
Which is bound tightly, supportively
Around evil's cerebellum
     the bin
In which we chuck all hate and vengeance
That [Key Lime] can go [Pie] himself in the [Yogurt]!

Speed

You saying my wrists
Are like hummingbirds on crack
Pink ceaseless buses?

Cedar Waxwing

Who hasn't loved
late winter berries
a little too well

curlicued off branches
hammered into snowbanks
only a tuft left to tell

we do it again
imbibe, fly loopy
for we need to be cradled
now and then

plucked forth plastered and
swaddled in Carhart
rocked til the heaving settles
til the headache takes wing

so toast me when the ice melts
hold me close in bare branches
here, far from the nest

Eggnog

Another year has passed, and still you remain
Like a pale, crusty flower from Christmas'
Wintry funeral.
Ominously, the bony white of your
Sloshing insides
Fends off the impending date of destruction.
You crouch behind Aunt Jemima,
A remnant of your former self.
   It is time for a cleansing,
   Time for a fresh start –
   But it is hard to let go…
For beyond your caked, yellow exterior
Your bitter, not-quite-right aroma,
I can still taste the sweetness
Of a snow-clad home
Swirling with warm light and
Cozy thoughts by the fireside.
You are a brooding relic now,
A tombstone to mark the passing
Of another holiday season.

Hound Dog Tayloring Along

Hound Dog Tayloring along

Only to note

Sun stayed out late last night

Still carousing

Bouncing off rooftops

And windowless sidewalls

Waiting for something

Blue blue blue

Basslines served up

Hair of the dog

I'm off to make finance

I say

He stops staggers leers

Half-slobbers downfence

And makes clear:

I do not give one shit

Bird 1506

one white stands
storm-wracked
solitary

- with whom to dance?

Ultralights, philanthropy
delicate flying house of cards
crash to a Floridian
pile of ivory feathers
milkweed fluff
soaked
downed
tangled
strewn in wet broken grass

one white stands
breathing opaline
alone

-    who returns with him
to the gathering of waters?

Leopold's ghost
weeps in silence
radio collars, high tech
fruitless in the whirl
of borders crossed
and ancient ways reopened

one white stands
winged capsule
rarity of rarities

-    who bugles back?

one white stands
long neck arced
out beyond hope

POSH

V-8s have an affinity for me
I am sun in an SUV
solar system, the center holds
They are drawn to me
as I stand manning the portcullis
subserviently, smiling, Jedi-like
in my regal nonchalance;
I tractor beam them in
Escalades, Navigators, Yukons –
all desire to cower before me.
I prepare for the reception of emissaries
my legs firm as the fieldstone columns
brow high and shining as the gables
I await the homage due to me:

When a burnt out Georgian
housewife, her covey in tow, inquires about
the pool

Big Golden

In mid-March

I finally met him

The gargantuan reactor

Above

We talked

On the rotten hay pudding

Clumped, swirled in front

Its plastic wrap

Of snow being partially removed.

He said God had hired him

Back in the day

To direct the rainbow pact with Noah.

But, he said smirking,

He'd also made the flood.

I glanced sidelong around me.

Already runnels ran

Furrowing crystal epoxy

Flipping deluge switch

To "on".

I wished him luck, a bit nervous

With unemployment on the up

But he replied

That prospects were good

For summer.

Dog Days

We painted the front door

Bright pink that summer

Just to piss off the neighbors

- It worked

Mr. Hubbard gave our cat

.22 acupuncture

And charged for parking

On his side of the street.

He waved his fist

On hot afternoons

- Something about property value -

We kept playing in the garage.

Then came brother's birthday.

Aunt Jane arrived

In her shamrock Volvo

Under a tired August sun.

She parked right in front

Of Mr. Hubbard's sign.

We rushed to open our bubblegum door

A crack

As Aunt Jane

Pounded through his sign

Red-faced

To Mr. Hubbard's house

And slammed both fleshy fists

On his elegant front door.

Frosting dripped unnoticed from my piece of cake

As Mr. Hubbard met

His first customer.

Swig

They drink Corona
-    and I drink Baltimore

Barely bitter enough
To counteract crab

Saltier than a deer lick
Grotesque on newspaper-
Sheathed picnic tables

I am not 21 yet
Sun shines behind rowhouses
Sweltering 3rd of July
Cracking claws
Navigating yellowish innards
- Damn that beer tastes good

Cheating Death

Write your last verse

From the banquet table

In the back of the hearse –

Hey, he, I owe you and sometimes why?

Your cuneiform takes time

So we'll read it backwards from the forty yardline

Since the ziggurats know Ur sacked.

Careful with your base,

Don't let the acids splash up in your face,

A cloistered world through rows of rose glasses

Raise the black lid

And upend the procession as the white walls skid

- Your words can cook pavement, boy

Be Not Afraid
Listening to Kamakawiwo'ole

The wave crests
I lunge, grabbing as it thrashes white away
Back into green
I have leapt off of my own accord
Under a tangerine slice
Setting sun

I am a distant smile
Bobbing with a lone ukulele
Plucking bittersweet

Having swum out
Ferociously seeking a view of every shore
Land is gone
Here, adrift, treading
With Neptune hair

Up the nostrils
Like a childhood taffy in the Dells
There's salt in the smile

Farewell, tablets and parchments
Granite markers, trophies, plaques and medallions
Even the smallest poem
Flutters down below

Languid notes
Comfort plucking along
Stars shake out endless tresses
The tied rope grows restless

Gaze, son, look up
The albatross about your neck
Struggles forth splashing
Leaving you breathless

Up in gentle breezes
I am hanged high
Wings casting feathers
A veil swirling down the night

Quiet smile
Every shore revealed

What General Jackson Saw

"At 4:00 in the morning, yeah, the whippoorwills are going and the doves are barking by then."

4:00 marks the barking of the doves
in eerie magnolia redoubts
high on ornate canyon walls;

a Japanese man in blue jeans cannot understand
the otherworldly sounds he hears,
cringes at the incoherent cackling of dark bushes,
and hopes Hitchcock was not
of the line of Isaiah

for leaden beaks click maliciously,
glinting coldly in faraway streetlights
    -    he bolts

the nervous, downy shuffling dies in silence
momentarily;
he is too slow
turning back at the silence,
the tautness of snowy legions perched
on every twig and granite ledge

in that instant, the moon escapes the clouds
revealing ten thousand thoughtless BBs
glimmering in the unmoving leaves

with a tremendous roar
the avalanche descends

Red Shift

I'll paint it as I see it

Rage red smoking quivering

Bridge, Giverny ablaze

Monet with cataracts

Fuming frustrated barely undaunted

Lilies glowing with toxic heat

Japanese in its last moments

A rouge roar over

Cataract of total annihilation

Though the lenses grime and smoke

I look not away

Let the brush shudder

I ignite my canvas

Antares sears the willows

I thought of you

And the scene lit

With vicious dark light

That few suspect lies

At the center of a star

Isle Hustle

DJ Straight Edge
Gonna come fuck you up
Gonna burn down Pavilion
Sans alphabet soup

Rage on night boardwalk
Rage on old Grove
Rage on pink croptop
Rage on cool pool

DJ Straight Edge
Gonna spin back your trysts
Gonna smoke your old pics
Til the cops come back

Fume under smile hoods
Fume at foot in mouth
Fume through the self song
Fume at dark sunrise

DJ Straight Edge
Gonna sweat it all out
Gonna calm it on down
Think sassafras swim swans

Bristle on the harbor dock
Bristle at the words
Bristle over table sparring
Bristle in the vacant stares

DJ Straight Edge
Gonna shoot rounds of fireballs
Gonna stow my last stand
Gonna sniff my stargazers
    -    Take you by the hand

Room, The Slanty Shanty

From "Swan Song or Life Thus Far"

If I shouldn't be alive
When the Robins come,
Tell them to scour the slanting space
For every last scrap,
The binders, the boxes, the stacks
Long in hibernation, closed like stone,
These Valves of my attention –
They have held back the real me,
Volumes, booklets, piles
Of poetry

    Much Madness is divinest Sense –
    To a discerning Eye –
    And so are these, these words of mine
    That never witnessed, lie

    I'm Nobody! Who are you?
    Are you – Nobody – Too?
    Having lived your life in parchment,
    Cryptic tales of things denied

Tell the Truth, but tell it slant –
Success in Circuit lies
Too bright for our infirm Delight
The Truth's superb surprise

    I wear white, though I wonder if this avatar
    Of virginity
    Is little more than
    Surrender, should I –
    Fight? Shall I row at last in Eden?

I heard a fly buzz when I died
And desperately I hoped
That he would tell them in
The Bustle in a House

The Morning after Death
- not to throw my life away

He questioned softly "Why I failed?"
"For Beauty," I replied –
"And I – for Truth – Themselves are One - "
And I knew then that it was done
Again, my life closed twice

Curtains

I have a terrible headache
Please turn out the light

'Tis well
Jefferson lives –
I have no regrets

Water,
Scrimshaw, make it stop

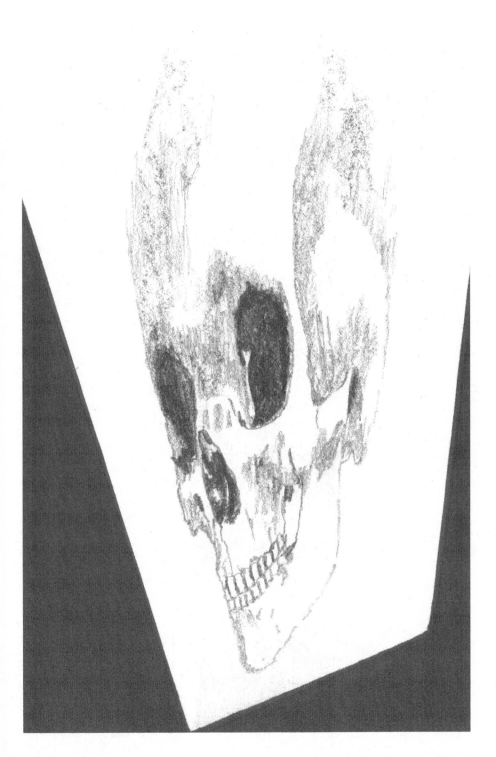

~ CLUES ~

Zen

Blue Jay:	Near Millhome
July:	Elkhart
Chief:	911
Fire Wheels Whir:	Perahera
Living:	Below the dam
Encapsulating Time:	The Cottage
Goblin Valley:	Nearly a second time
Bell Captain's Stand:	Ivy and green roofs
44th, Vanderbilt, and Madison:	Midtown
Spring:	Hillcrest
The Bittersweet Mysteries:	UWRCF
Something Borrowed:	The Parker
Blackout Clash:	Back field
From a Tower in Hong Kong:	CC
Picking Stones:	Champion
Mocha Velvet Bottlebrush:	Delaware River
Written in the Dark:	Isthmus

Iris *Originally appeared Menagerie, EWC publication, c. 2002 and "The Streets of Kiel and Other Poems"

Nachtmusik:	Dorm
Mellification:	A real practice

Feathers

Cry of the Indigo Bunting:	Along the ditches
Montgolfier:	Hot air balloon ride
Diamonds:	Albano

Having Met Life: Watch for the shadow

Indelible Tea (In the Pines):   A story briefly told

Strangled: Central City

By Water: Deck, Blackhawk Island

Marsh: Above the railroad trestle

Neutral Ground Runners: NOLA

Tamarack: Walla Hi

Eine Cline: Several weeks communicating solely in haiku

Red Ostrich Feathers in the Living Room: Inside the Footprint

Quake Before the Lord: Jericho, Long Island

Surviving the Salt Mines

Where There is Smoke: Lakeland College, a premonition

Terminal City: GCT

42nd Floor: Interview

Never Touch the Stuff: Poetry as an alternative

Too Many Irons Smother A Fire: Kiel Marsh

FOB, Fear of Breaking: Contracts with Ponoroff

March at the Firm: March was always the worst

Prayer to My Patron: It is possible

Charon's Yellow Skiff: Heading home late

Progress: Belgian settlement

Kilimanjaro: Hemingway

Tunnel's End: Former site of Air Fort

Crazy Talk

The Health Benefits of Temporary Insanity: Air Hockey

A Defense of Love: In the style of a poet I cannot recall

Semi-Abstract Angry Musings: The War on Terror

Speed:	Gesticulations
Cedar Waxwing:	Capitol Square
Egg Nog:	Home, MKE
Hound Dog Tayloring Along:	Murray Hill
Bird 1506:	Whooping Cranes
POSH:	Lola's place
Dog Days:	Hillcrest and Mueller
Swig:	Thanks, Bryan
Be Not Afraid:	Read along with Somewhere Over the Rainbow
What General Jackson Saw:	Feeling Hitchcocky in D.C.
Isle Hustle:	Ha
Room, The Slanty Shanty:	Poetry manuscripts in a metal box
Curtains:	Last words

**A number of the poems herein were originally compiled by Shari Vogel into the collection "Words from Within" as a personal gift to the poet.

About the Poet

At various points a reporter, bellhop, busker, legislative aide, blogger, political cartoonist, historic preservation fellow and finance lawyer, Brad Vogel grew up in Kiel, Wisconsin. He began writing poetry in earnest in fourth grade. Vogel graduated from the University of Wisconsin at Madison with degrees in Journalism and Political Science, and later earned his law degree at Tulane. Vogel and his boyfriend Suresh reside in New York City.

Made in the USA
San Bernardino, CA
06 January 2016